From Field

To Fly

The Fly Tier's Guide to Skinning and Preserving Wild Game

Scott J. Seymour

From Field To Fly

Scott J. Seymour

Frank Amato
PORTLAND

Acknowledgements

There are a number of people who need to be thanked, some of whom were directly involved in helping to make this book a reality and some of whom are more indirectly responsible in one way or another.

First, many thanks to Frank Amato for doing for me what he has done for many, many writers before me. Frank gave me a chance by enthusiastically agreeing to publish my very first book.

Next, I would like to thank my good friend Hugh Wabers who not only was my photography consultant on this book but years ago introduced me to fly fishing and taught me much of what I know about our fine sport. His friendship as well as our short fishing expeditions have meant a lot to me over the years. I look forward to future fishing excursions when our busy schedules and family obligations permit it. I also need to thank Gene Knutson who donated his time to photograph all the flies in this book. Gene has even been gracious enough to share the location of a favorite fishing hole or two.

I would also like to thank Bob Harrison, who could be described as no less than a local legend for his fly fishing and tying prowess as well as his ability to flawlessly deliver the punch line to any joke. Bob not only tied all of the flies in this book but also opened up his personal fly fishing library to me. He also reviewed the book and provided a number of suggestions which I have incorporated. While Hugh taught me most of what I know about fly fishing, Bob taught Hugh most of what he knows on the subject. Hugh and I will continue to pester him for valuable tidbits of information which he might choose to throw our way.

I would also like to thank Art of Art's Taxidermy for discussing his trade with me. I hope to re-pay him by continuing to deliver trophies to his shop, should I be so lucky.

Now, to thank those who did not directly contribute to this book but who have influenced it nevertheless.

I would like to thank my mother for encouraging me to write over the years and my father for taking me bird hunting at a very young age which sparked my love for the outdoors. Of course, I am thankful to my parents for much more than this but do not have the time and space here to do them justice.

Without my hunting experiences, I doubt that I would have had the interest or motivation to write this book. For this reason, I must thank my old friend Geoff Klos, his father, Jerome, and brother, Bryant, for inviting me seventeen years ago into what can only be described as the finest examples of traditional American duck and deer hunts.

I would certainly be remiss in failing to thank Robert Doyle for, albeit unknowingly, giving me the idea for this book.

Last, but certainly not least, I thank my wife, Vicki, for her amazing patience and understanding in allowing me to pursue my many and varied passions over the years.

Dedicated to my wife, Vicki, and daughters, Melissa and Ashley

◆

Photography: Scott J. Seymour
Fly Plate Photography: Gene Knutson
Fly Tying: Bob Harrison
Design: Jerry Hutchinson
Cover Art: Dürtin Kampmann

ISBN: 1-57188-205-7

© 2000 Frank Amato Publications, Inc.
P.O. Box 82112, Portland, Oregon 97282
(503) 653-8108
Printed in Singapore
1 3 5 7 9 10 8 6 4 2

Foreword

✦━━━✦

Foreword

The idea for this book was born from a rather innocuous discussion I had one day a number of years ago with a fellow fly fishing fanatic on a picturesque stream in southwestern Wisconsin. As I recall it, Robert and I were having what started out as a friendly conversation about one of my upcoming fall duck hunting adventures on the Mississippi river south of Lacrosse, Wisconsin.

I was describing what amazing success I had been having on this annual trip for many years, taking a variety of waterfowl including mallards, widgeon, teal and wood ducks, when Robert rudely interrupted me. "What do you do with the birds?" he demanded. I began to explain how we first fillet the breasts and then we wrap them in bacon, cut up some onions and apples, salt and pepper to taste and then wrap them in tin foil for the grill when I was again interrupted. "Not the meat, the feathers you idiot!" Robert blurted, completely disrupting the tranquillity of the moment.

Upon lecturing me of my sinful ways for what seemed like hours, Robert explained how he had been searching all summer in various fly shops and mail order magazines for a wood duck skin that did not cost an arm and a leg. That's when it hit me like a ton of bricks. I had been an avid hunter all my life, harvesting a wide variety of game including deer, turkey, grouse, pheasant, quail, squirrel, rabbit, etc.

From that day on, I vowed that I would learn how to prepare and preserve game which I had taken in the field for tying flies. Upon searching libraries, book stores and every other resource I came across, I soon realized there were no such books out there which were written with the fly tier in mind.

Most of what I have learned on the subject has come from consulting taxidermists, reading books written for individuals pursuing a career in commercial taxidermy as well as talking to other fly tiers and, of course, from trial and error. The methods for preserving game which are described in this book are not the only methods which can be used but I believe they are the safest, easiest and most practical from the fly tier's point of view.

This book is not designed to make you a better fly tier or fisher. There arewritten for the amateur fly tier looking for a resource to help them prepare and preserve wild game suitable for the vise. You certainly don't have to be a hunter to take advantage of this book. One doesn't have to look far (especially in fly fishing circles) to find a hunter who would be more than willing to part with an animal carcass which is going to be put to good use. Most likely, that hunter will be flattered by the inquiry. In fact, hunters may well be lining up at your front door once they realize you are willing to clean their bounty at no charge.

Of course, there are other ways to collect game. For example, fresh road kill. Unfortunately, those rare opportunities seem to arise only on trips when my wife happens to be present in the car. I have never been able to convince her that it would be worthwhile to stop. Oh well, happy hunting, as they say.

Chapter 1
Introduction

About the Book

Since its inception, the art of fly tying has been accomplished with natural fur and feathers. While, in recent years, there has been an explosion of synthetic materials never before seen in our sport, there are still many who believe there is and never will be a man-made substitute for natural materials. In his book, *Fly-Dressing Materials*, John Veniard noted "If you want to imitate nature—use nature". I don't mean to suggest that synthetics are not useful. They have more than proven their effectiveness while adding a new element of creativity, providing potentially limitless supplies of unique materials in varying colors which simply do not exist in nature. Synthetics have also replaced natural materials which are no longer available. Many tiers, including myself, routinely combine natural materials with synthetics to produce extremely successful flies. However, by themselves, these materials often fall short in their ability to mimic the life-like qualities of fur and feathers.

We know that to create flies that produce the desired results, color and movement are important. Most food items preyed upon by trout have earthtone colors which can also be found in a wide variety of North American birds and animals. Although some colors, such as red, are believed to stimulate strikes, we generally attempt to match the color of insects and aquatic life indigenous to the waters we fish. For these reasons, I tend to choose natural over man-made materials.

The purpose of this book is to provide a basic resource for fly tiers which describes how to inexpensively clean, prepare and preserve wild game for the tying bench. In addition, I will attempt to identify, generally, those parts of wild game which I and many other fly tiers have commonly incorporated into flies which have proven to be successful over and over again. Specific recipes for various patterns can be found at the end of each chapter. They include both popular and less known but equally effective flies. Of course, all of the flies referenced in the book incorporate wild-game materials.

By no means should the flies referenced in the book be considered an all-inclusive list. There is not and never should be such a list. Most would agree that one of the great joys of tying your own flies includes improvising and creating new versions that actually catch trout. In addition, the reality is that as further species become threatened, the fly tier will need to adapt, utilizing animals which happen to be available at the time which may not have been commonly used before. Although many species continue to decline in numbers, there are some animals such as the white tail deer and Canada goose which have actually experienced a dramatic increase in numbers due, in part, to changing logging and farming practices. The resourceful fly tier will undoubtedly capitalize on these positive changes in our environment when they occur, devising new patterns from the more abundant species.

Obviously, different parts of birds and animals contain vastly different properties. How these materials are ultimately utilized can vary greatly from one fly tier to another. You might discover uses for feather, fur, and hair which no one before you ever contemplated. Such experimentation can be extremely satisfying, especially upon catching your first fish with a new creation. Anyone who ties flies can probably remember with vivid clarity catching that first trout on their own fly. For me, catching trout on flies which I have tied using game which I have taken in the field simply takes "the thrill" to another level.

Several years ago, I was fishing a popular small spring creek near my home. Due to heavy fishing pressure that day, I camped out on a narrow, deep hole which usually held fish. A mayfly hatch came off but there was no feeding at or near the surface. I fished an appropriate sized dark Hare's Ear Nymph and Pheasant Tail Nymph without success. Eventually I took notice that the mayflies were significantly lighter in color than the nymphs which I'd been using. I tied on a light-colored nymph constructed from a ruffed grouse taken during the previous hunting season and proceeded to pull more than a dozen fish out of the hole on nearly as many casts. This and other similar episodes continue to motivate me to experiment with wild game materials.

Of course, when you do invent a new fly which is successful, it is advantageous to be able to duplicate it. For years, serious fly fishermen have kept detailed notes on flies they have created for this very reason. Specific species of wild game can vary greatly from one specimen to another. For example, an individual ruffed grouse can vary greatly in color from a multitude of shades of red, gray, and brown. If you want to recreate a fly that works for you, you should become familiar with the Borger Color System (BCS). This is essentially a color chart designed by Gary Borger to help fly tiers identify 147 shades of color using numerical references. The chart is useful not only for duplicating flies but for identifying insect color in the field, as well.

I have broken down chapters in this book by various animal and bird groups. This has been done not just for the sake of simplicity. At the risk of stating the obvious, techniques used to clean and prepare one type of bird or animal can generally be applied to other birds and animals within that same group. However, while the skinning and preservation of a ring-necked pheasant, ruffed grouse and woodcock might be identical (and amazingly simple), the same techniques might not necessarily be ideal for waterfowl such as mallards or wood ducks. The instructions and photographic illustrations should provide you with easy-to-follow directions. The rest is up to you.

Tools

There is good news for the fly tier who has already spent a small fortune on numerous tools and gadgets, many of which are designed for a sole, minute purpose. The few tools needed to skin and preserve a bird or animal are readily available in most households.

A pair of medium-sized tin snips or poultry bone cutters which can be purchased in any hardware store is a must for cleanly cutting through bone, cartilage, and tendons of birds and small game.

A small filet type knife with a sharp point is advisable particularly for piercing the skin and making the initial incision. (While a scalpel is ideal for this purpose, it is by no means essential).

A dull, yes I said dull, pairing knife is recommended particularly for removing the skin from large mammals. Using a sharp knife for this purpose increases the likelihood of cutting through the hide or into the meat, something which we don't want left on the skin. All meat and fatty tissue will need to be removed to prevent microscopic organisms from destroying the hide and to ensure that it is properly preserved.

A spoon can also be a handy tool for scraping fatty tissue from the skin of birds or animals.

You will need to construct a fleshing beam out of a 2 X 6 piece of wood (or smaller for skins from small game). This is quite easy and is described in more detail in Chapters 5 and 6.

A box of tacks are useful for flattening out skins on a sheet of cardboard or plywood during the drying process.

Tools

Once again, if not already available in your household, most of the products needed for drying and preserving skins can be found in your local grocery, lawn, and garden or hardware store.

Salt

Un-iodized salt is used, particularly on large animal skins, to help draw moisture from the hide and slow the decaying process before tanning. Table salt, or any fine grain salt for that matter, works just fine.

Borax

Borax is used primarily for drying and preserving bird skins. It is quite effective in warding off unwanted insects and is relatively inexpensive. At one time, it was also used for preserving small game skins as well. I would not recommend it for anything other than bird skins as it will not completely cure thicker skins, leaving them (and possibly other valuable tying materials) susceptible to infestation and decay.

A small amount of borax is also called for in some of the preserving solutions suggested in this book. 20 Mule Team borax, which can be purchased in any grocery store, is quite satisfactory.

Cornmeal

Borax is normally used on birds during the skinning process to prevent unwanted body fluids from running on to the feathers. However, if the bird meat is going to be consumed (I can't imagine harvesting and not eating a grouse or pheasant, they are truly delicious) cornmeal should be substituted for borax during the skinning process.

Sawdust

When it is necessary to wash skins in detergent to clean them or to rinse after being immersed in a degreaser or other solution, sawdust is an excellent drying and fluffing agent to restore hair, fur, and feathers to their original state.

Household Detergents

Just about any kind of household detergent, when diluted in warm water, is suitable for removing blood, dirt, grime, and body fluids from animal and bird skins. I normally use Dawn dishwashing liquid for this task.

White Gasoline/Camping Fuel or Mineral Spirits

Some bird skins, like certain species of waterfowl, and animal skins, such as beaver and muskrat, can be quite greasy or fatty. White gasoline (camping fuel) or mineral spirits can be used to remove these substances from the skin. All of these degreasers can be found at your local hardware store in the section where solvents and paint thinners are sold.

Preserving Chemicals

Denatured alcohol or commercial grain alcohol and aluminum sulfate are needed in varying quantities and combinations for the preserving process. Denatured alcohol can be found in any hardware store in the same area as the degreasers, and aluminum sulfate can be purchased at most lawn and garden stores or farmer co-ops as it is typically used as a soil conditioner. Easy-to-follow recipes are given for various preserving solutions throughout this book. Like any potentially dangerous household chemicals, they should be kept safely out of reach when not in use.

Chapter 2
Birds

I would personally rate bagging a grouse in the thickest of cover or downing a duck traveling from right to left at 45 miles an hour with taking a rising, finicky trout which carefully inspects your fly before inhaling it. All are equally challenging as well as exhilarating. When I am not able to pursue these worthy quarry, I can usually be found at the tying bench, devising flies from animals taken in the field. We are fortunate to live on a continent which truly has an abundance of feathered game which can provide a limitless and inexpensive supply of tying materials.

The earliest evidence of man's efforts to produce an artificial fly dates back to 400 B.C. These simplistic creations were amazingly similar to some of the hackle-less flies still being tied today. While techniques for fastening feathers to hooks has changed somewhat over the centuries, we still use feathers to construct wings and tails on countless numbers of fly patterns. A few of them will be described later on.

Skinning Versus Plucking

You may be wondering why you should even bother skinning birds when it might be less time-consuming, you might think, to simply pluck those feathers called for in more common fly patterns and then discard the remainder of the bird. There are two valid reasons for skinning and preserving the entire bird.

First, skinning versus plucking may actually save you time in the long run. Once the basic techniques are learned, you will be able to skin and preserve a bird in less time than it will take you to pluck and then individually label and store each group of feathers in separate bags or storage containers. These bags or containers may become quite numerous depending upon how many species you intend to collect, only adding to the confusion and delay involved in locating and selecting the feather you need. In addition, over time tying materials have a tendency to become disorganized, making it difficult to identify individual feathers when they become separated from their labeled containers.

In contrast, once the bird is preserved and completely dry, it (with the exception of larger species such as turkey and geese) can be stored anywhere as long as the environment is clean and dry. There is no need to label since having the entire skin intact will allow you to easily recognize the species. You can then pull the appropriate sized feather from the skin after comparing it to others, knowing exactly where to find the breast feather, flank feather or whatever type of feather it is you are searching for.

The same logic can be applied to animal skins as well. For example, gray squirrel skins possess several colors other than gray. They include cream and white fur on the under belly, a strip of olive coloration along the back as well as a rusty brown color on the head. Having the entire skin available will allow you to inspect it and then select and snip off the colors which you need for a specific pattern.

The second and perhaps more important reason for retaining the entire skin is to encourage the fly tier to improvise and be creative. If only those feathers which are called for in more common patterns are retained, the opportunity to examine the bird for equally useful but often overlooked feathers is lost. This would be unfortunate since experimentation is the hallmark of the art of fly tying.

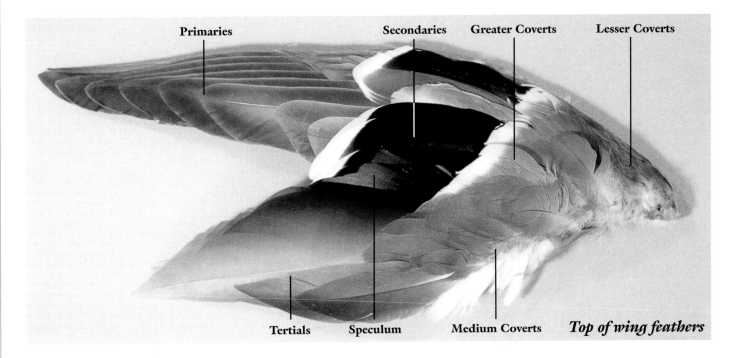

Primaries · Secondaries · Greater Coverts · Lesser Coverts

Tertials · Speculum · Medium Coverts · *Top of wing feathers*

Identifying Game Feathers

In order to tie various patterns which call for specific game feathers or to be able to consistently reproduce your own patterns, it is helpful to be able to identify those feathers. This is far less complicated than some might think. At the risk of oversimplifying, feathers from game birds can be classified into three groups: wing feathers, body or contour feathers and tail feathers.

Wing Feathers

Primaries: (also known as "pointers") are the long, pointed feathers located at the wing's tip. These, as well as the secondaries, are often

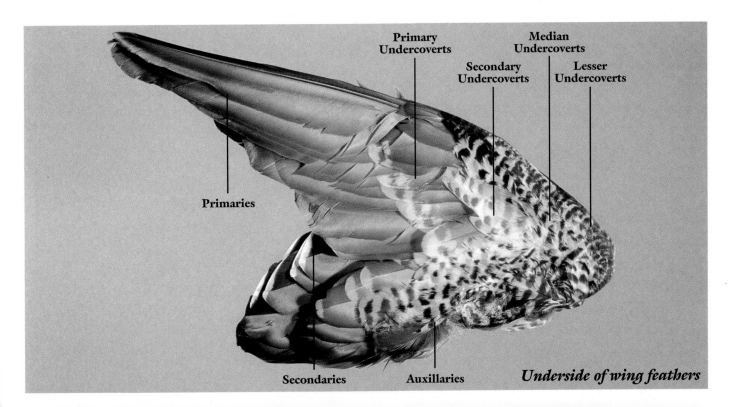

Primary Undercoverts · Median Undercoverts · Secondary Undercoverts · Lesser Undercoverts

Primaries

Secondaries · Auxillaries · *Underside of wing feathers*

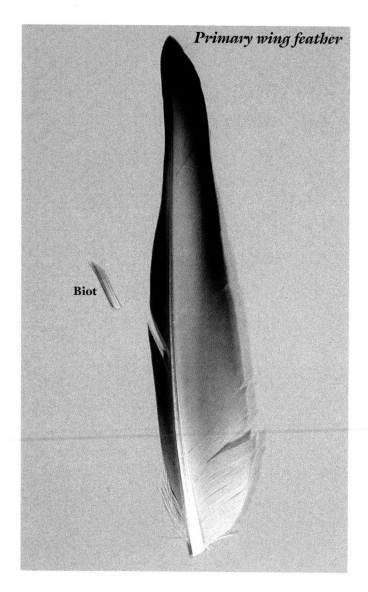

Primary wing feather

Biot

referred to as wing quills. They are commonly used as wing material.

A number of patterns call for the use of goose and turkey "biots". These are the barbs located on the short side of the primary wing feather from geese or other large birds. Biots are often used for tails or antennae or are wrapped to construct the abdomen on a number of dry-fly patterns.

Secondaries: (Also known as "flight" feathers) are the shorter feathers located closer to the bird's body. Like primary feathers, these are also used for wing, tail, and leg material.

Coverts: These feathers have traditionally been used for soft-hackle (wet) flies which were popular many years ago. The effectiveness of these flies appears to have been rediscovered as they are once again gaining in popularity.

The cupped feathers located on the leading edge of the wing are used for winging mayflies such as the Pale Morning Dun found at the end of Chapter 4. These feathers are commonly referred to as "shoulder" feathers.

Undercoverts: These feathers can be used for palmering hackles as well as constructing tails and legs. On waterfowl, the underside of the wing has layers of fine-textured feathers which have been used for fly wings. These feathers are known as "satinets".

Body (Contour) and Tail Feathers

Neck: If stiff enough, these feathers can be used as hackles for dry flies.

Breast, Belly and Rump: Make good marabou, soft hackles.

Flank: Used for tails and wings of dry flies as well as legs of nymphs.

Back: Can be used to construct wings of grasshoppers as well as hackle of mayflies, again, if the fibers are stiff enough.

Tail Coverts and Tail Feathers: Good wing, tail and leg material. Some tail feathers such as the cock pheasant tail as well as the ruffed grouse tail are used to create bodies and wing casings as well.

Marabou: A soft, fluffy, down-like, weak shafted mass of feather branches found beneath body feathers next to the skin. Marabou found on wild turkey legs is particularly well suited for tying the Marabou Leech and similar patterns.

Aftershaft: A soft feather varying in size which is attached to a body feather at its base. If large enough, these feathers can be used as substitutes for marabou. They also make excellent soft hackles. Aftershaft feathers are commonly misidentified as filoplume feathers which are described next.

Filoplume: A minute, hair-like feather which has feather branches only at the tip found growing in clusters around the follicles of some body feathers. These feathers are more difficult to locate than aftershaft feathers. As a result, aftershaft feathers are often substituted for filoplume feathers.

Cul De Canard: This is a soft wispy feather found on waterfowl which is located at the oil or preen gland just in front of the tail coverts. It makes good wing material for emerger and dry mayfly patterns. The oils on these feathers make them naturally buoyant.

While the above provides a very basic description of how many feathers are often used, it cannot be stressed enough that these, as well as other feathers not specifically identified, can and should be experimented with by the fly tier. By having the entire skin available for inspection, the tier can easily select the feather with the properties desired for the task at hand.

Although there are some exceptions, most game birds do not possess the uniquely stiff fibers which most fly tiers have become accustomed to in tying hackled dry flies. This is not surprising given that many suppliers have turned to genetically engineered strains of birds cultivated solely for purposes of producing high-quality hackles. However, such expensive, hard-to-find hackles are not always necessary to create successful dry flies.

Authors Doug Swisher and Carl Richards, in their highly acclaimed book, *Selective Trout*, suggest that typically hackled dry flies create an unnatural appearance from the fish's viewpoint by making the least significant feature of a fly (the legs) the most significant feature. Sparsely tied, hackle-less flies with wings constructed of such materials as duck shoulder, wing quill feathers, or deer hair and bodies made of various types of fur such as rabbit which are treated with floatant to produce more realistic profiles which, they maintain, are more effective than traditional dry-fly patterns. My own experiences with such flies in slower waters which receive a lot of fishing pressure have only confirmed their theories.

Chapter 3
Upland Game Birds

Pursuing upland game birds is one of my favorite pastimes. Like catching trout with your own flies, there is a great deal of satisfaction in watching a dog which you have patiently trained staunchly point a pheasant, hold until it is flushed, and ultimately retrieving the bird to hand.

In this chapter we will describe how to skin and preserve upland game birds. Upland game birds, simply put, are birds which spend the vast majority of the time on land as opposed to waterfowl which spend a large percentage of their time on water, typically migrate to warmer climates in winter and have webbed feet. To name just a few, upland game birds include pheasant, grouse (ruffed, sharp tail, sage, blue, etc.), Hungarian partridge, quail, dove, and turkey. There are a few birds which are difficult to classify such as the woodcock which prefers land over water and does not have webbed feet but follows the same migratory habits as waterfowl.

Generally speaking, feathers of upland birds have different properties than those of waterfowl. While some individual feathers such as wing quills are used for dry flies, overall, upland game feathers tend to be softer and are more inclined to separate, making them more suitable for wet flies. Waterfowl feathers, on the other hand, tend to naturally repel water and individual fibers of some feathers do not separate as easily, making them ideal for dry flies.

Skinning and Preserving Upland Game Birds

The process of successfully skinning and preserving any game begins with proper field care. Freshly killed game should be skinned as soon as possible. Shortly after being killed in the field, birds which you intend to utilize for fly tying should be placed in a cool, dry, and clean environment until they are skinned. It is also a good idea to place cotton in the bird's beak as well as in any sizable wounds as soon as possible to keep body fluids from leaking onto the feathers. Use cold water and a cotton ball to wipe any fresh blood off the feathers before it has time to set. Ideally, the bird should be cleaned after it has cooled but within several hours after it is killed. Any hunter or taxidermist will tell you that virtually every animal is easier to skin the sooner the task is undertaken. This is generally so because the skin begins to shrink shortly after death. Sometimes it is not possible to skin an animal soon after killed given the location and duration of a particular hunt. If it becomes apparent that the bird cannot be skinned within several hours after killed, it should be placed on ice or in a refrigerator. If the bird cannot be cleaned within 24 hours, it should be wrapped in an air-tight plastic zip-lock type bag and frozen whole and then thawed slowly in a refrigerator before skinning.

An upland game bird is probably the easiest of all animals to skin. Therefore, it is a good animal to start out with if you have not done it before. With a little practice you will soon be skinning game with ease. Fortunately, if a few small mistakes are made along the way they are of little consequence in comparison to the taxidermist whose job it is to create a near perfect, life-like replica of a living creature. The fly tier need only ensure that a skin is clean and well preserved since the purpose is to use the feathers over time

Having dispensed with the preliminaries, we are now ready to skin the bird. We begin by laying the bird on its back, breast side up on a table or other flat surface with the tail pointing towards you. Using a filet knife or pocket knife with a sharp tip (or a scalpel if you have one), make an incision from the top of the breastbone down to the anus, being careful to cut only the skin and not the meat or intestinal wall beneath it. There is a line which runs along the center of the bird's breast where feathers typically do not grow. It is along this channel that the incision should be made to preserve as many feathers as possible. If you intend to preserve the head feathers, you can go back and extend the incision from the breast along the underside of the neck until you reach the beak. **Figure 3-1.**

Once the initial cut is made, gently work the skin on both sides of the incision toward the legs, wings, and tail thereby exposing the breast meat and belly area. On most upland bird species this step can be accomplished with your fingers rather than a knife. **Figure 3-2.**

Before proceeding any further, you should sprinkle a liberal amount of borax on the exposed areas of the bird to prevent body fluids from finding their way on the feathers. This should be done periodically as the skinning progresses. If the bird is an integral part of your dinner plans (I have no idea why one would not intend to consume a game bird) you should use cornmeal instead of borax until you have completely separated the skin from the body.

Next, using a pair of tin snips or game cutters, snip off the feet just above the area where the feathers end on the legs. **See Figure 3-3.**

Now, gently pull the legs up through the skin, completely freeing them. **Figure 3-4.**

You are now ready to separate the tail section from the body. To do this, work the skin down to the base of the tail. To free the tail section from the body, sever the base of the tailbone just in front of the feather roots, being careful not to cut through the skin on the back. **Figure 3-5.** If you intend to keep the tail section permanently attached to the rest of the skin (I recommend

Figure 3-1

Figure 3-2

Figure 3-3

this except on very large species such as geese or turkey) it is important not to cut through the feather roots as this will cause the feathers to fall out eventually.

Now that the tail section has been freed, work the entire skin forward towards the wings. At times, it may be necessary to cut the tissue away to avoid tearing the skin. Although not necessary, some taxidermists find it easier to complete the skinning process from this point by tying a cord around the exposed body and hanging the bird upside down at eye level.

When you reach the wings, like the legs, work the skin toward the base of each wing and sever the wing bones with a bone cutter or tin snips. **Figure 3-6.**

Continue to pull the skin forward until you reach the head. **Figure 3-7.** If you wish to preserve the skin covering the head, continue to peel the skin up to the beak, cutting around the eye sockets if necessary, and then cutting the skin away from the beak, completely freeing it from the body. If the skin does not peel easily over the head, it will be necessary to extend the incision from the breast/neck area all the way up to the base of the lower beak. If you don't wish to preserve the head feathers, simply make a circular cut around the neck area to free the skin. The skinning process is now complete.

Before preserving, if the bird is heavily soiled or blood stains have set before they can be wiped away, it may be necessary to wash the entire skin by immersing it in a gallon of cold water containing one to two teaspoons of liquid detergent and allowing it to soak for 10 to 15 minutes. (Dawn dishwashing liquid works as well as anything.) Remove the skin, rinse in plain water and then gently squeeze out the excess water, working from head to tail.

To dry the skin, first gently press it down on a few newspapers to absorb as much water as possible. Next, tumble it gently in a paper bag filled with sawdust. You may need to replace the sawdust more than once. Then dust the feathers with several handfuls of borax. These agents can be removed from the feathers by gently beating the skin with a switch and

Figure 3-4

Figure 3-5

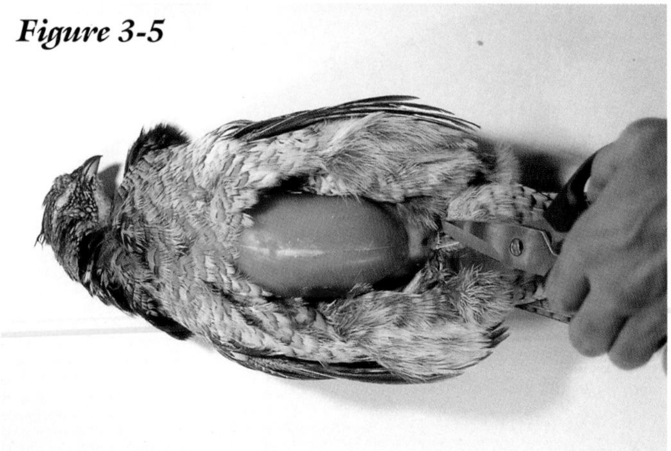

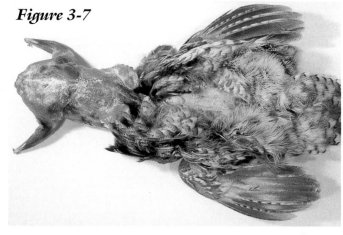
Figure 3-6

Figure 3-7

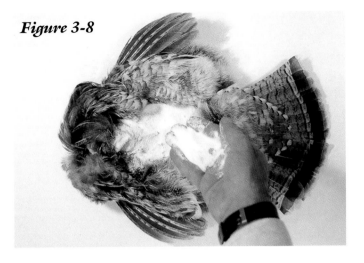

Figure 3-8

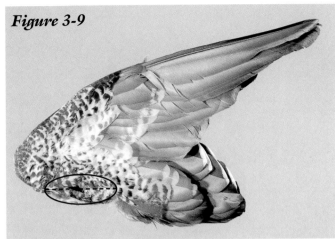

Figure 3-9

then using a blow dryer (with little or no heat) to remove the remainder.

To begin the preservation process, lay the skin on a flat surface feathers down, skin side up. With a dull knife or spoon, gently scrape any remaining meat or fat from the skin. When scraping, always do so towards the head to avoid tearing the skin. You will also need to revisit the wing and tail sections to cut away any remaining fatty tissue or meat. Now rub liberal amounts of borax into these areas as well as the rest of the skin and leave it alone for 24 hours. **Figure 3-8.** The borax will dry out the skin. It also acts as a tanning agent, toughening the skin, as well as an insecticide. After 24 hours, gently beat the skin to remove as much borax as possible, reapply borax to the skin and let it sit for a week or two.

To ensure that the wings are adequately preserved it is also advisable (particularly with larger bird species such as geese or turkey) to make two incisions along the outer and middle sections of the wing bones on the underside of the wing as shown in **Figure 3-9.** Now strip away as much meat as possible along the wing bones and apply borax to the area.

After the borax has been applied for a week or so, you can either tack the skin, feather side up, to a piece of plywood or cardboard so the bird dries out with a flattened form, or simply lay the skin on a flat surface, feather side down, resulting in a skin which dries with a slightly rounded form. After the skin has completely dried out in several weeks or so, beat it gently once again with

a switch and brush the skin lightly with a soft bristle paintbrush to remove any remaining borax. You now have a completely preserved bird skin which can be stored or even displayed until it is needed for fly tying.

Pheasant skin

Grouse skin

wing cases. However, they can also provide the fly tier with an infinite variety of shapes, sizes, and colors to choose from for devising traditional, contemporary, and experimental patterns.

When treated with floatants, upland bird feathers can be used to construct wings and tails of dry flies with exceptionally good results. I fully anticipate that these underutilized but plentiful birds, once considered unsuitable for dry flies, will receive increasingly more attention in the coming years.

Below is a sampling of personal favorites which utilize upland game feathers in one way or another. Some are very popular and are fished universally while others are less known but have nevertheless proven their effectiveness under the right conditions. It is important to note that the same insect species can vary greatly in color, size, and shape not only from one region to another but from streams within the same geographic area. Don't be afraid to substitute materials called for in specific patterns. If you have just taken up fly tying, the prospect of creating your own patterns may seem out of reach. However, once you have learned the basic techniques in constructing nymphs, emergers, wet, and dry flies, you will find that all it takes is a little imagination to tie your own unique flies with wild game which is available to you in your area. The more skins you accumulate over time, the easier it will be to match the size, shape, and color of your local hatches.

If you are a beginning fly tier, I recommend two very good references: *Fly Tying Made Clear and Simple* by Skip Morris and *The Art of Fly Tying* by John Van Vliet. Both books provide excellent instructions on basic techniques.

None of the fly patterns referenced in this book contain recommended hook types and sizes or thread size and color. I believe these details are a matter of personal preference. The only suggestion I would make is that the idea here is to match the hook size and thread color to the naturals which you are attempting to imitate.

Some feathers will inevitably become bent and ruffled during the hunt, or perhaps during the cleaning and preserving process or after they have been carelessly packed away in storage. Some of these feathers may appear to be so badly disturbed that you will be tempted to discard them. Before doing so first try applying steam to the feathers to restore them to their original form. A teapot can be used for this purpose but I have found that my wife's hand-held garment steamer works exceptionally well. You will be amazed at the results.

Fly Patterns

Feathers of upland game birds have been used primarily for dressing wet flies with soft hackles and nymphs with legs, tails, abdomen, and

Pheasant Tail

Tail: Pheasant tail fibers
Rib: Fine copper wire
Body: Pheasant tail fibers wrapped herl style
Thorax: Peacock herl
Note: Grouse tail can be substituted for pheasant for lighter pattern with more distinct light/dark contrast

Breadcrust Nymph

Rib: Stripped grouse tail feather
Body: Rabbit dubbing
Hackle: Ruffed grouse body hackle

Quill Gordon Nymph

Tail: Pheasant tail fibers
Rib: Brown thread
Body: Beaver dubbing or similar
Wingcase: Mottled turkey wing quill
Thorax: Same as body
Beard: Brown partridge feather

Caddis Pupa (Gary Borger)

Abdomen: Fur dubbing to match natural
Thorax: Same as above with guard hairs
Hackle: Grouse body feather, lesser covert coot or chukkar or under coverts of woodcock
Note: Borger mixes sparkle yarn with dubbing.

Peeking Caddis

Rib: Fine oval gold tinsel
Body: Natural rabbit dubbing
Thorax: Olive rabbit dubbing
Beard: Ring-necked pheasant back feather fibers
Head: Black dubbing from squirrel, muskrat, beaver, etc.

Sparrow

Tail: 1 or 2 short "marabou" ring-necked under rump feathers
Body: Gray squirrel with guard hairs blended with gray rabbit under fur
Collar: Hackle mottled gray and brown pheasant rump as a folded hackle
Head Hackle: One or two gray pheasant after shaft feathers as a folded hackle

Grouse Nymph

Tail: Ruffed grouse tail fibers
Body: Gray grouse aftershaft tapered
Ribbing: Stripped grouse tail center quill
Thorax: Tannish down from base of tail
    feathers
Wingcase: Section of fibers from black tip of
    grouse tail pulled forward

Philo Thorax

Thread: Red
Tail: Grouse hackle barbs
Thorax: Hare's ear fur
Abdomen: Grouse philoplume, wrapped
Legs: Grouse hackle applied as a collar

Mostly Pheasant

Tail: Pheasant tail barbs
Abdomen: Gray aftershafts tied in by butts and
    wrapped forward
Rib: Gold wire
Thorax: Peacock herl
Legs: Pheasant back feather
Wingcase: Pheasant church window feather
    coated with cement
Wingcase: Pheasant church window coated with
    vinyl cement and pulled forward

American March Brown

Tail: Mottled grouse hackle fibers
Rib: Oval gold tinsel
Body: Grayish tan rabbit dubbing
Wing: Mottled turkey quill segments

Carey Special

Tail: Male ring-necked pheasant rump fibers
Body: Peacock herl wound with gold wire
Hackle: Male ring-necked pheasant rump
    feather

Pheasant Leech

Tail: Dense bunch of filoplume from
    ring-necked pheasant
Body: Dark gray or brown dubbing
Wing: Same as tail

Partridge & Green
Thread: Black
Body: Bright green silk floss
Collar: Brown or gray partridge hackle

Woodcock & Orange
Thread: Brown
Body: Orange silk floss
Collar: Woodcock body feather

La Fontaine's Caddis Larva
Body Case: Grouse body feather wrapped over yellow thread and trimmed to shape
Body: Pale yellow dubbing
Thorax: Same as body
Legs: Dark brown or gray grouse hackle barbs

Marabou Leech
Tail: Natural gray turkey marabou
Body: Same marabou as tail
Thorax: Dubbed marabou
Head: Bead head optional

Egg Laying Caddis
Body: Dubbing to match natural
Wing: Light elk over which is a collar of dark grouse body feather trimmed away from bottom
Antennae: 2 long pheasant tail barbs

Quail Jassid
Body: Thread to match color of natural
Hackle: Matched to natural, palmered, trimmed on top and bottom
Wing: Quail breast feathers tied flat over body

Chapter 4
Waterfowl

Fly fishers and duck hunters have far more in common than they realize. They all long for cloudy, rainy days in hopes that such miserably wonderful weather will somehow increase their chances of success on the stream and in the field. They also recognize that ducks are an extremely valuable resource worth preserving. Organizations such as Ducks Unlimited and Trout Unlimited have donated a great deal of time and money to improving our environment, only recently has it begun to have a positive effect on waterfowl populations which have been decreasing due to declining water quality and loss of wetlands. Despite their overall decline, ducks fortunately are still relatively abundant throughout most of the North American Continent.

Skinning Waterfowl

You already know how to skin a bird so I will not repeat those steps again here. I would note that skinning waterfowl can be, depending upon the species, somewhat more challenging than upland birds so it may take a bit more time your first few tries. The difficulty arises from the fact that the skin does not separate as easily from the body as it does with upland game, particularly around the legs, tail, and back area. When this occurs during the skinning process, simply cut the skin away from the body with a sharp, pointed knife tip (like that on a filet knife) and contin-

ue on. Once you get the hang of it, you will be able to skin waterfowl nearly as quickly and easily as upland birds.

Preserving Waterfowl

For some reason, the skins of waterfowl tend to be much greasier than other birds. I would hazard a guess that this relates in some way to their incredible ability to withstand extremely cold, wet climates. To properly preserve them we need to incorporate a few extra steps beyond what is described in Chapter 3.

After skinning, lay the bird on a table skin side up and scrape off any fat, tissue, meat, etc from the skin with a spoon or dull knife. Once again, be sure to scrape from tail to head.

To degrease the skin, simply immerse it completely in white gasoline (camping fuel) or mineral spirits which can be found at your local hardware store. (Note: These chemicals should only be used in a well-ventilated area as they are flammable.) Allow the skin to soak for no more than five minutes, remove it and then gently squeeze out the excess solution, working from head to tail. The mineral spirits or camping fuel can be reused as the dissolved fatty deposits will sink to the bottom of your container, allowing you to pour the clear solvent back into the original container.

The skin should now be washed by allowing it to soak for fifteen minutes in a gallon of cold water containing a teaspoon of liquid detergent. Remove the skin, rinse in plain water, and then gently ring out the excess water, again working from head to tail and dry using the method described in Chapter 3.

If you are concerned that immersing the entire skin in the degreasing solution might strip away natural oils from the feathers, potentially affecting their buoyancy, saturate the skin only with the degreasing solution and allow it to soak into the skin for ten minutes before washing and rinsing as noted above. I have not noted a significant difference in buoyancy between feathers immersed in a degreaser and those that are not. However, this could be due to the fact that I apply floatant to all of my dry flies shortly after tying them.

After drying, you are now ready to finish preserving the bird by rubbing liberal amounts of borax into the skin, allowing it to sit for 24 hours and then reapplying borax once or twice over a two-week period. After that, gently beat the skin to remove any loose borax and set the skin aside or tack it, feather side up, to a piece of wood or cardboard and allow it to dry out for several weeks. When the skin is completely dry, brush away any remaining borax and display or store as desired.

Fly Patterns

Waterfowl feathers have probably been incorporated into more fly patterns than any other wild-game material. There is a good reason for this. These feathers are naturally buoyant and tend to stay married better than feathers of other birds, making them easier to tie and more durable.

Primary and secondary quills have traditionally been used for winging various wet and dry flies and body feathers have been used for creating legs and tails as well as wings. Of particular interest to fly tiers are the uniquely barred markings of mallard, teal, and most notably, woodduck flank feathers which are known as "fly tier's gold". Also of interest to the tier are the cul de canard (CDC) feathers located near the preen gland on a duck's rump. These wispy, naturally repellent feathers can mimic the vein-like qualities of mayfly wings and have been used as wings on wet, emerger, dun, and spinner patterns.

Dark Hendrickson Nymph

Tail: Woodduck flank fibers
Body: Muskrat
Rib: Fine silver wire
Thorax: Same as body
Wingcase: Dark brown duck or goose
Legs: Same as tail

Light Cahill Nymph

Tail: Woodduck flank fibers
Body: Cream rabbit
Thorax: Same as body
Wingcase: Mallard flank fibers
Legs: Same as tail

BWO Nymph

Tail: Woodduck flank
Body: Olive rabbit
Thorax: Same as body
Wingcase: Goose wing quill fibers
Legs: Brown partridge hackle

◆

Gray Fox Nymph

Tail: Brown mallard breast fibers
Body: Dark and light brown rabbit fur, mixed
Wingcase: Turkey quill segment
Legs: Same as tail

Feather Leg Nymph

Tail: Mallard, teal, or woodduck flank to match natural
Body: Dubbing to match natural
Wingcase: Iridescent green or blue feather from neck of pheasant or mallard, lacquered
Legs: Same as tail

Gray Caddis Pupa

Body: Muskrat
Rib: Brown leader material
Wing: Mallard quill segments
Legs: Gray mallard flank fibers
Head: Ostrich herl

Wet/Dry fly

Tail: Sparkle yarn to imitate nymphal shuck
Body: Dubbing to match natural mixed
  with sparkle yarn
Hackle: Marginal covert feather from coot,
  mallard, wood duck to match natural

Quill Winged Olive

Tail: Woodduck flank fibers
Body: Olive and gray muskrat
Wings: Paired mallard wing quill, slanted
  back

No Hackle Mayfly

Tail: Stiff fibers tied in forked
Body: Dubbing to match color of natural
Wings: Duck wing quill segments to match
  natural

◆

CDC Biot Comparadun

Tail: Stiff fibers tied in forked
Abdomen: Goose or turkey biot, wrapped
Wing: CDC with mixed mallard or
  woodduck flank

Pale Morning Dun

Tail: Light olive hackle fibers
Body: Pale yellow and light olive beaver
Wings: Light gray duck shoulder

Duck Quill Caddis

Tail: None
Hackle: Dubbing to match natural
Wing: Duck quill, tied-in tent style

Chapter 5
Small Game

Squirrel and rabbit hunting occupy some of my earliest childhood memories of days afield. Pursuit of these small game animals taught me how to shoot straight. Now that I think about it, I could probably use a refresher course. Little did I know at the time that these animals provide excellent dubbing material for wet and dry flies. The guard hairs also make good tail and wing material.

In addition to squirrel and rabbit, there are a wide variety of small game animals which make perfectly good fly tying materials including (but not limited to) fox, opossum, woodchuck, muskrat, and beaver. Like waterfowl, muskrat and beaver—which spend most of their time in or around water—have natural oils which tend to make their fur naturally water repellent and, thus, ideal for dry flies. However, as noted earlier, when treated with floatants, just about any natural dubbing material obtained from small game animals is suitable for dry flies.

Skinning & Preserving Small Game

Skinning small game is not unlike skinning birds. We begin by laying the animal on its back and making an incision from the top of the breast bone to the tail. **Figure 5-1.** Now work the skin to the sides, exposing as much of the front and hind legs as possible. **Figure 5-2.** Snip the front and back feet off with tin snips or game cutters. **Figure 5-3.** Now, make an incision along the inseam of each leg and then pull (or cut, if necessary) the skin from each leg. **Figure 5-4.** Continue to work the skin around the hind quarters and pull the tail bone completely out of the tail section. **Figure 5-5.** With some animals such as squirrels, the tailbone

Figure 5-1

Figure 5-2

Figure 5-3

may not come out easily. It may be necessary to make an incision along the entire length of the underside of the tail to free the tailbone. Now, simply work the skin forward toward and then over the head and finish by cutting the skin from the skull. **See Figure 5-6.**

Scrape off all fat and tissue from the skin with a spoon or dull knife. Like waterfowl, muskrat and beaver tend to be quite greasy. They should be immersed in mineral spirits or white gasoline (camping fuel) for approximately 2 hours to degrease them.

Whether degreased or not, the skin should now be rinsed in a gallon of water which contains a teaspoon of liquid detergent to remove any remaining dirt, grime, or blood. After squeezing out the detergent water, scrape the skin again and rinse in plain water. It is now ready to be preserved.

To preserve the skin, simply immerse it in a solution of full-strength denatured alcohol for at least 48 hours in a plastic or glass container with a tight-fitting lid. (A family-size plastic pickle jar works well.) Otherwise, the alcohol will evaporate rapidly. The skin can actually be left in this solution without being damaged for up to a month. Denatured alcohol can be found at your local hardware store near the solvents and paint thinners.

Upon removing the skin from the alcohol, it should now be rinsed in a gallon of water containing 4 ounces of dissolved borax. Rinse again in plain water and then squeeze out the excess water. Press the skin between two newspapers to further remove water and then tumble it first in sawdust and then in borax to fluff the fur and repel insects. A blow dryer set on low heat can be used to speed the drying process. Flatten out the skin by tacking it to cardboard or plywood and allow it to dry out completely. As the skin dries, it will harden and shrink somewhat. Store as desired.

Zonker Strips

The preserving process outlined above results in a "pickled" rather than tanned skin. The "pick-

ling" process is the easiest and quickest method of preserving small animal skins. If the skins are going to be used primarily for dubbing, wing, and tail material, I recommend the "pickling"

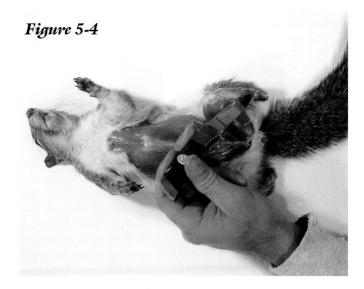

Figure 5-4

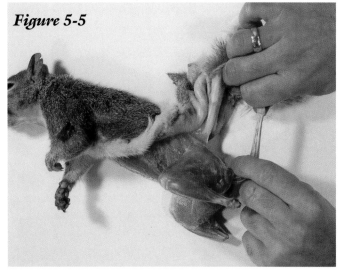

Figure 5-5

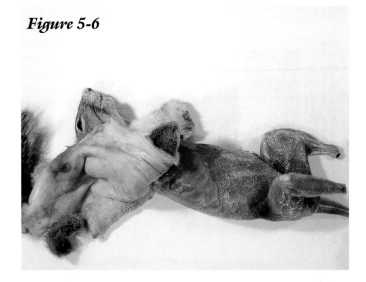

Figure 5-6

process. However, a pickled skin will not be soft and pliable. If you want to preserve a rabbit or other skin for purposes of creating zonker strips to tie the Zonker, Dahlberg Diver, or similar patterns, it will need to be tanned. This is not difficult. It is simply a bit more time-consuming.

After the animal is skinned, it will need to be scraped, washed, and immersed in denatured alcohol as outlined in the previous section. Upon removing the skin from alcohol, you will need to "work" the skin on a fleshing beam. A fleshing beam can be constructed by tapering, sanding the edges, and rounding one end of a 1 X 4-inch piece of hardwood and then sanding it to give it a smooth finish. **See Figure 5-7.**

The beam will then need to be clamped, bolted, or fastened in some manner to a bench or sawhorse. Now pull the skin over the rounded end of the beam and scrape the entire skin with a knife that has at least a six-inch blade much like you would scrape the bottom of a tennis shoe to remove gum from the sole. Be careful not to cut the skin. (Note: You may want to create a second handle with a block of wood, insert the tip of the knife into it so that you can scrape the skin by applying pressure evenly on the blade with both hands.) This

scraping has the effect of breaking up the skin fibers which will allow the tanning solution to penetrate the skin. **See Figure 5-7.**

After the skin has been thoroughly scraped, soak it in a solution containing a gallon of soft water, a half cup of aluminum sulfate, and a half cup of un-iodized salt for several days or until the skin turns an even white color all the way through. Use a plastic or glass container with a tight-fitting lid. You will need to use hot water when mixing the formula to fully dissolve the salt and aluminum sulfate. Allow the solution to cool before placing the skin in the solution to avoid cooking it. As noted earlier, aluminum sulfate can be obtained at your local hardware or lawn and garden store or a farmer's co-op as it is often used to condition soil.

After it turns white, remove the skin, wring it out, and then soak it for ten minutes in a pail of water containing 4 ounces of dissolved borax. The skin should then be rinsed thoroughly in plain water. Rub and stretch the skin until it is soft and dry. This can be done by working the skin over the edge of the fleshing beam in the same manner as you would polish a shoe with a strip of cloth. To further soften the skin apply Neat's Foot Oil to the skin, as well.

Figure 5-7

To make Zonker strips, simply lay the skin on a table, hair side down and cut the skin with a razor blade.

As you have already seen from fly patterns listed in previous chapters, fur from small game animals makes excellent dubbing material. Dubbing can easily be created by clipping or shaving hair from the preserved animal skin and then using a coffee grinder to chop and blend the material to the desired consistency. Use the grinder for short intervals, checking the dubbing material frequently. If ground to long, dubbing will eventually be reduced to a powder substance, rendering it useless for tying. I would recommend purchasing a separate grinder as your significant other will not likely appreciate the grinder's multiple uses beyond preparing coffee beans for the morning brew.

The softer underfur located near the skin of the animal is ideal for dry- and wet-fly dubbing.

The guard hairs should be pulled from the skin before shaving or clipping the hair to create fine-textured dubbing. However, the guard hairs should be left in to create "bugginess".

Small game animals can supply the fly tier with dubbing in a wide variety of natural colors. For example, the gray squirrel alone has not only several shades of gray, but cream and white fur on the underside, a strip of olive-colored fur along the back as well as rust-colored fur on the head.

Rabbit skins, in particular, can be easily dyed by the novice in a wide variety of colors. Although I tend to select natural material and blend them to create variations in color, there are some patterns which require dyed material by necessity. In her book, *Fly Tying Tools and Materials,* Jacqueline Wakeford provides instructions on how to dye fur and feathers as well as deer hair. In *Dyeing and Bleaching,* A.K. Best does the same in even greater detail and also has a chapter on how to blend dyed rabbit dubbing to create 19 different colors.

Hare's Ear
Tail: Hare's mask guard hairs
Rib: Gold or copper wire
Body: Hare's mask dubbing
Wingcase: Turkey, goose, or mallard wing quill

Gray Squirrel Nymph
Tail: Gray squirrel guard hairs
Abdomen: Gray squirrel body fur, including guard hairs
Rib: Silver wire
Thorax: Same as abdomen with fur picked out
Wingcase: Cemented turkey tail

Red Fox Squirrel Hair Nymph
Tail: Red squirrel guard hairs
Rib: Fine gold tinsel
Abdomen: Underfur from orange-tan area at base of tail of red squirrel
Thorax: Red squirrel underfur with guard hairs

Sow Bug

Tail: Gray goose biots
Rib: Fine silver wire
Body: Muskrat dubbing
Legs: Fibers picked out on sides

Mueller's Muddler

Tail: Gray squirrel tail
Body: Flat tinsel
Underwing: Same as tail
Head: Spun deer hair

Hair Leg Scud

Body: Blended hare's mask, red fox squirrel
and tan sparkle yarn
Rib: Copper or silver wire
Shell: Latex

◆

Cottontail Muddler

Tail: Brown rabbit fur
Body: Flat gold tinsel
Wing: Same as tail
Collar: Rabbit guard hairs with underfur left
in tied with spinning loop wet-hackle style
Head: Ball of dubbed rabbit underfur

Dahlberg Diver

Tail: Rabbit fur strip
Topping: Flashabou
Collar and Head: Deer hair spun and
clipped to shape

Zonker

Tail: Mylar
Body: Silver Mylar tubing
Hackle: Brown grouse body feather
Wing: Rabbit fur strip

Chapter 6
Deer (And Other Large Game)

Remaining perfectly still as a large whitetail deer approaches you while maintaining even a semblance of control over your nerves to take a steady shot is every bit as exciting as hooking a trophy rainbow trout on a size-20 hook.

The North American whitetail deer is truly an awesome creature. It is no wonder that, once harvested, it can be put to so many good uses, from providing delicious table fare to making high-quality leather products such as gloves and coats. And, of course, deer hair has a wide variety of fly tying uses which will be examined more closely at the end of this chapter.

Fortunately, deer are abundant throughout the entire continent. In Wisconsin alone, there are over 400,000 deer harvested by hunters every year and yet populations continue to grow. The fly tier does not have to look far to get his hands on one of these fine hides.

There are other large game animals which make good fly tying material as well, such as moose, elk, antelope, and bear to name just a few. However, these hides can be a bit more difficult to obtain.

Skinning Large Game

Before skinning (and before field dressing for that matter), remove the tail by cutting or snipping through the tailbone at its base with a sharp knife or tin snips. Make a slit along the

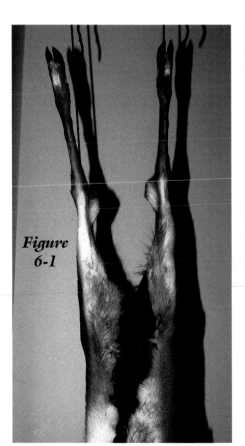
Figure 6-1

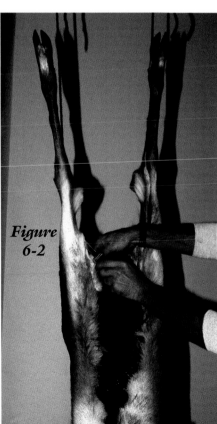
Figure 6-2

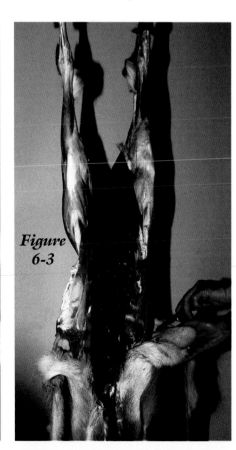
Figure 6-3

tailbone on the underside of the tail and completely remove it. Apply borax to the exposed area and allow the tail to dry out for a few weeks.

To skin a deer or other similar animal it is easiest to hang the animal from its hind legs. **Figure 6-1.** It will most certainly have been field dressed at this point. You will now want to cut the skin along the inseam of each leg. **Figure 6-2.** If you wish to skin the entire head, extend the incision from the breastbone area all the way up the neck to the jaw.

Once the above incisions are made, go back to the hind legs and begin the actual skinning process by making a circular cut around each hind leg several inches below the hooves. Now peel the hide downward. Use a dull knife to cut the skin away from the body only when it appears that the hide is not separating cleanly from the meat. You can use a pair of pliers to grip the edge of the hide to aid in pulling the hide downward. Continue working in this fashion until you reach the head. **Figures 6-3, 6-4, and 6-5.**

If you do not wish to preserve the hair on the head simply make a circular cut around the base of the neck to completely free the hide from the body. Otherwise, continue on until reaching the nose and end of the lower jaw area. After the hide is completely removed, you will need to skin out the individual ears, removing the cartilage completely to ensure that the hide is properly preserved.

Preserving Large Game

After skinning, allow the hide to dry out somewhat for a 24-hour period. This will allow you to scrape fat and flesh from the hide more easily. A butter knife can be used to do this. Once the hide has been completely scraped, lay it on a flat surface, hair side down, and apply liberal amounts of un-iodized salt to the skin. This will slow the decaying process and draw moisture from the hide. Now fold the hide over on itself (hair on the outside), roll it up, and store in a cool, dry place for another 24 hours. One end of the roll should be propped up to allow moisture to drain out of the lower end. After that, unroll the hide, scrape off the old salt, re-apply more salt, roll up again and set aside for another 24 hours.

If you cannot get to the hide within the next day or two, put it in a garbage bag and place it in a freezer. Thaw the hide out in the refrigerator when you can get to it again.

The next step in the preservation process involves "fleshing" the hide. This procedure was already discussed in the previous chapter in explaining how to prepare a rabbit skin for purposes of making Zonker strips, page 27.

Before fleshing, wash the hide with water to remove any

Figure 6-4

Figure 6-5

remaining salt. If the hide has dried out and become stiff, you will need to soak it in water to soften it. You can throw in a handful of borax to speed up the softening process. As soon as the hide has softened, remove it from the water and begin the fleshing process. Don't soak it too long as this will result in hair slipping from the hide.

You may want to construct a fleshing beam which is larger than the one used to flesh rabbit skins. A two-and-a-half-foot-long, 2X6-inch piece of wood is suitable for deer hides. As already indicated, the purpose of fleshing is to reduce the thickness of the hide and break up the skin fibers which will allow the tanning solution to penetrate the hide. Place the hide over the fleshing beam, skin side up. The pointed or tapered end of the beam should be facing your stomach. You will want to lean up against this end of the beam to hold the skin in place while pushing the knife away from you. To flesh the hide, use a sharp knife with a blade at least eight inches in length and insert the tip of the knife

into a block of wood like a second handle so that you can apply even pressure on both ends of the knife. **See Figure 6-6.** As stated earlier, the technique involved in fleshing is similar to scraping gum off the bottom of a tennis shoe with a knife. There is a thin, elastic membrane over the skin which must be removed during the fleshing process. Once you have scraped or fleshed the entire hide thoroughly, completely immerse it in the following solution:

In two gallons of hot water, dissolve 5 pounds of salt, 1 1/2 pounds of aluminum sulfate, and 4 ounces of borax in a large plastic pail or drum with a tight-fitting top. Allow the solution to cool before immersing hide.

Allow the hide to soak in this solution from three days to one week, until the skin turns a uniform white color throughout. Rinse the hide thoroughly in plain water and then hang it, allowing it to drip dry. The drying process can be accelerated by tumbling the hide in wood chips.

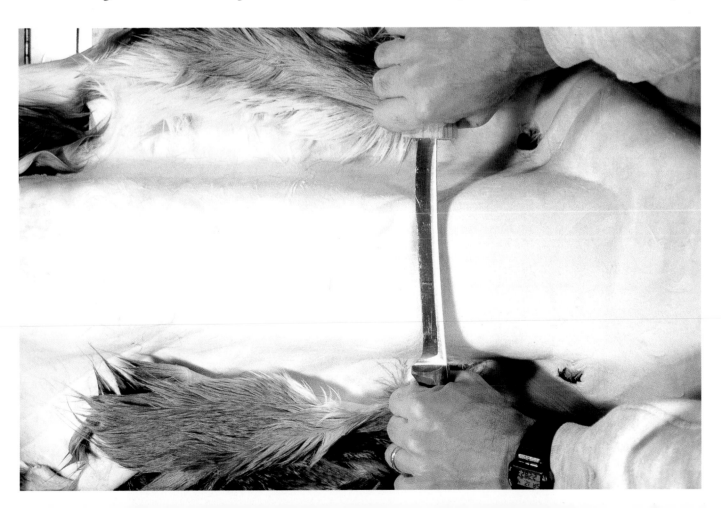

You may want to cut the hide into smaller sizes to make them easier to store. This should be done before the hide has completely dried. Use a razor blade or carpet knife and make cuts on the skin rather than the hair side. To keep the hide in a flattened state, the individual pieces should be nailed or tacked to a piece of plywood, skin side up, until it dries completely.

Fly Patterns

Deer hair (as well as elk, caribou, and other similar animals) is a unique and versatile material. It is used to create wings and tails on a wide variety of patterns. Individual body hairs contain unique air cells which make it buoyant and also cause it to flare when spun around a metal hook. Deer tail hair, on the other hand, is not hollow and its kinky, or wave-like, nature gives lifelike qualities to streamers, salmon flies, and other similar fly patterns.

Body hair from the back and underside of the whitetail deer is generally used for spinning. The longer neck hair is more often used on streamer-type patterns. Leg and mask deer hair is excellent for tails and wings of smaller patterns such as the Comparadun featured on page 36.

Most of the patterns in this chapter call for whitetail deer hair. I have selected these patterns for this chapter only because the whitetail deer happens to be the most widely distributed and abundant big-game animal on the continent. However, hair from similar big-game animals can and should be substituted in these as well as many other patterns. For example, individual elk-hair fibers are quite stiff and firm and are excellent for creating wings, tails, and antennae on a number of well-known patterns, such as the Elk Hair Caddis. Moose hair is sought after by many fly tiers for tailing material as it is very stiff and coarse. Antelope and caribou body hair is said to make very good spinning material although I have not had the pleasure of trying it myself. Each individual animal can provide a wide variety of colors. A Wisconsin hunter who took a successful trip to Montana recently provided me with several

swatches of hide taken from an elk cow which he had harvested. I was truly amazed by the wide variety of colors which included shades of tan, orange, black, and brown. That elk hair was fished this season in the form of the Hair Wing Dun pattern to match a local *Hexagenia* hatch. It was responsible for hooking the largest trout I have ever caught in Wisconsin waters.

You may not be lucky enough to know an elk hunter. However, on your next roadtrip maybe you will be fortunate enough to happen upon a very large, fresh roadkill. It would be a shame to let it go to waste. Don't be shy. Skin the desirable parts of the hide. After reading this book, you know exactly what to do with it.

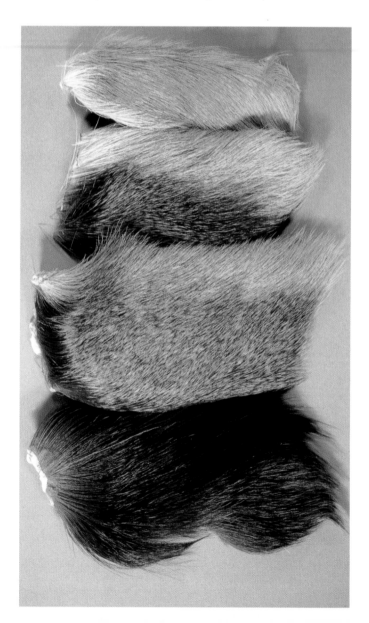

Devil Bug

Tail: Deer or other similar hair to match color of emerging caddis
Back: Same as above
Underbody: Dubbing to match natural. Olive is shown above

Sculpin

Rib: Brass wire
Body: Light colored dubbing
Wing: Gray squirrel tail
Pectoral Fins: Ring-necked pheasant rump
Collar/Head: Gray deer hair

Muddler Minnow

Tail: Mottled turkey wing quill
Body: Flat gold tinsel
Wing: Gray squirrel tail with turkey wing quill sections tied over that
Head/Collar: Spun deer hair

Madam X

Tail: Natural light deer body hair
Body: Fluorescent orange or yellow floss
Head and Wing: Same as tail, tied in reverse or bullet-head style
Leg: White or yellow to form an X

Dave's Hopper

Tail: Looped yellow yarn
Body: Same as tail
Hackle: Brown, palmered and clipped
Wing: Turkey wing quill segmented, lacquered
Legs: Pheasant tail fibers, clipped and knotted
Head and Collar: Natural deer hair, spun and clipped

Deer Hair Mouse

Tail: Long brown-and-white barred grouse undercovert feathers or leather strip
Body: Natural deer or similar hair clipped to shape

Black Nose Dace
Tail: Red yarn
Body: Flat silver tinsel
Rib: Oval silver tinsel
Wing: White bucktail, dark bucktail, and
    then brown bucktail

Hi Tie
Tail: Bucktail
Wing: Stacked bucktail with Krystal Flash

Troth Skater
Body: Tying thread
Hackle: Deer hair or similar, tied fore and
    aft

Comparadun
Tail: Hackle or hair fibers
Body: Dubing to match natural
Wing: Elk or deer body hair tied upright

Hair Wing Dun
Tail: Clump of pheasant tail fibers
Body: Extended deer hair to match natural
Thorax: Dubbing to match natural
Wing: Deer or similar hair

Elk Hair Caddis
Body: Rabbit or similar dubbing to match
    natural
Hackle: Optional
Wing: Deer or similar hair to match natural

Chapter 7
Game Laws

While I am certain that the vast majority of fly fishers need not be reminded to adhere to state and federal game laws, nevertheless I feel compelled to do so anyway, given the content of this book, as well as my present occupation.

Rules and regulations relating to possession and bag limits of wild game vary greatly from state to state. It would be impossible to summarize these ever-changing laws here.

A "bag" limit generally refers to the number of animals which can be legally harvested in a day. "Possession" limits, on the other hand, refer to the total number of animals which an individual can possess in total. States typically require that certain animal skins only be acquired, transported, and possessed with a valid hunting license during designated hunting seasons. Some states allow for the harvesting of certain specified animals without a hunting license outside of regular hunting seasons under limited circumstances, for example, on a landowner's own property or to reduce populations of varmints or other animals which cause property damage.

In many states, roadkill of certain large game animals, such as deer, require that law enforcement officials be notified so an animal can be

properly tagged before any portion of it can be possessed or transported.

Obviously, certain protected species cannot be possessed under any circumstances. Such species can vary from state to state.

In addition to state laws, federal regulations also exist which restrict the possession and transportation of various species such as migratory game birds. For example, federal law prohibits the transportation of migratory birds without a wing or head attached to the bird until one reaches their primary residence.

Like rules which ensure healthy numbers of trout and other fish, these laws exist to help continue to sustain populations of birds and animals. It is our ethical responsibility as hunters and fishers to become intimately familiar with these regulations before collecting and accumulating animal skins.

Bibliography

Best, A.K. 1993. *Dyeing and Bleaching*. Lyons & Burford, New York, New York.

Borger, Gary. 1986. *Borger Color System*. Gary Borger Enterprises, Inc., Wausau, Wisconsin.

Borger, Gary. 1991. *Designing Trout Flies*. Tomorrow River Press, Wausau, Wisconsin.

Morris, Skip. 1992. *Fly Tying Made Clear And Simple*. Frank Amato Publications, Portland, Oregon.

Mueller, Ross. 1995. *Upper Midwest Flies That Catch Trout*. Palmer Publications, Inc., Amherst, Wisconsin.

Swisher, Doug and Carl Richards. 1971. *Selective Trout*. Winchester Press, New York, New York.

Van Vliet, John. 1994. *The Art Of Fly Tying*. Cy Decosse, Inc., Minnetonka, Minnesota.

Veniard, John. 1977. *Fly Dressing Materials*. Winchester Press, New York, New York.

Wakeford, Jacqueline. 1991. *Fly Tying Tools And Materials*. Lyons & Burford Publishers, New York, New York.

Gene Knutson

Gene Knutson photographed all of the flies in this book. Gene is an ophthalmic photographer at the University of Wisconsin Eye Clinic in Madison. He has been involved in photography for thirty years and has been fly fishing for the past six years. His only regret is that he didn't start fly fishing thirty years earlier.

Bob Harrison

Bob Harrison tied all of the flies featured in this book. He is a master fly tier and has been fly fishing for over 30 years. His father took him along on fishing trips when he was old enough to walk on his own and Bob has been walking up and down stream banks ever since. Like many Midwesterners, Bob started his career with bluegills and still considers them to be one of the most enjoyable fish one can pursue with a fly. He has pursued bonefish and sharks in the Florida flats and salmon in Alaska but spends much of his time fishing for trout, smallmouth, and pike in his home state of Wisconsin.

FLY PATTERNS FOR STILLWATERS

Philip Rowley

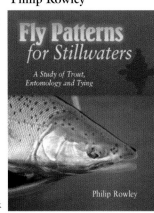

Phil has spent countless hours at lakes studying the food sources that make up the diet of trout; then set up home aquariums to more closely observe the movement, development, and emergence of the aquatic insects. In this book he explains the link between understanding the food base within lakes to designing effective fly patterns for these environs. Phil covers all major trout food sources for the whole year. He gives detailed information on each, plus how to tie a representative pattern and fish it effectively. Numerous proven stillwater patterns are given for each insect and include clear and concise tying instructions. This book will be a long-standing stillwater fly pattern reference for years to come. All-color, 8 1/2 x 11 inches, 104 pages.
SB: $29.95

TROUT FLIES OF THE EAST

Jim Schollmeyer and Ted Leeson

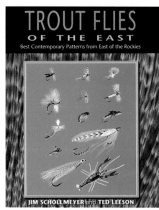

In fly fishing, there is no substitute for local knowledge. Walk into any fly shop and you will find "shop patterns"— flies local to the area. Far more often than not, these are the top choices for fishing rivers and lakes in a given area. Second in a series devoted to celebrating these flies, this book focuses on trout flies, although some are well-suited to steelhead, salmon, and warmwater species as well. Patterns shared include: attractors and multi-purpose; mayflies; caddisflies; stoneflies; midges; damsel and dragonfly, hellgrammite, crustaceans; baitfish; leeches; terrestrials; and more. Once again, Jim and Ted provide top-quality writing and photography. Your fly-fishing library is not complete without this first-rate book. 8 1/2 x 11 inches; 128 pages. All color.
SB: $34.95
SPIRAL HB: $44.95

FLY TYING MADE CLEAR AND SIMPLE

Skip Morris

Expert tier Skip Morris shows how easy it is to tie excellent flies in this all-color book. Over 220 color photographs show all the techniques you need to know. 73 different materials in color plus 27 tools. Clear, precise advice tells you how to do it step-by-step as well as pointing out difficulties and explaining how to overcome them! Dries, wets, streamers, nymphs, etc., included so that you can tie virtually any pattern. 8 1/2 x 11 inches, 80 pages.
SPIRAL SB: $19.95
HB: $29.95

TROUT FLIES OF THE WEST: CONTEMPORARY PATTERNS FROM THE ROCKY MOUNTAINS, WEST

Jim Schollmeyer and Ted Leeson

This beautifully illustrated, all-color book features over 300 of the West's best specialty trout flies and their recipes and an explanation of each fly's use. The flies and information were researched from scores of the West's finest fly shops. Over 600 color photographs. The very latest word on the most effective Western patterns! 8 1/2 x 11, 128 pages.
SB: $34.95

THE FLY TIER'S BENCHSIDE REFERENCE TO TECHNIQUES AND DRESSING STYLES

Ted Leeson and Jim Schollmeyer

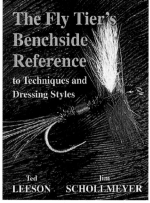

Printed in full color on top-quality paper, this book features over 3,000 color photographs and over 400,000 words describing and showing, step-by-step, hundreds of fly-tying techniques! Leeson and Schollmeyer have collaborated to produce this masterful volume which will be the standard fly-tying reference book for the entire trout-fishing world. Through enormous effort on their part they bring to all who love flies and fly fishing a wonderful compendium of fly-tying knowledge. Every fly tier should have this book in their library! All color, 8 1/2 by 11 inches, 464 pages, over 3,000 color photographs, index, hardbound with dust jacket.
HB: $100.00.

FEDERATION OF FLY FISHERS FLY PATTERN ENCYCLOPEDIA OVER 1600 OF THE BEST FLY PATTERNS

Edited by Al & Gretchen Beatty

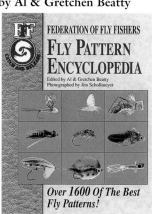

Simply stated, this book is a Federation of Fly Fishers' conclave taken to the next level, a level that allows the reader to enjoy the learning and sharing in the comfort of their own home. The flies, ideas, and techniques shared herein are from the "best of the best" demonstration fly tiers North America has to offer. The tiers are the famous as well as the unknown with one simple characteristic in common; they freely share their knowledge. Many of the unpublished patterns in this book contain materials, tips, tricks, or gems of information never before seen.

As you leaf through these pages, you will get from them just what you would if you spent time in the fly tying area at any FFF function. At such a show, if you dedicate time to observing the individual tiers, you can learn the information, tips, or tricks they are demonstrating. All of this knowledge can be found in *Federation of Fly Fishers Fly Pattern Encyclopedia* so get comfortable and get ready to improve upon your fly tying technique with the help of some of North America's best fly tiers. Full color, 8 1/2 x 11 inches, 232 pages.
SB: $39.95
SPIRAL HB: $49.95

Frank Amato Publications, Inc. • P.O. Box 82112, Portland , OR 97282 • (503) 653-8108 • 1-800-541-9498